Free With Every Pack

Robin Kingsland

Young Lions

Two Hoots	Helen Cresswell
Desperate for a Dog	Rose Impey
Free with Every Pack	Robin Kingsland
Mossop's Last Chance	Michael Morpurgo
Hiccup Harry	Chris Powling
Ging Gang Goolie – It's An Alien!	Bob Wilson

Published in Young Lions 1988
Second impression September 1988

Young Lions is an imprint of
the Children's Division, part of
the Collins Publishing Group,
8 Grafton Street, London W1X 3LA

Printed and bound in Great Britain by
William Collins Sons & Co. Ltd, Glasgow

Chapter One

'It's not fair!'

Waldo stared miserably at his
breakfast bowl, and at the little
plastic packet that lay on top of his
Hunny Poppers.

FREE WITH EVERY PACK.

it had said on the box,

ONE OF THESE AMAZING TOYS

and what had Waldo got?

Paper.

A measly little bit of folded-up paper.

'It's a stinking cheat!' he said,
banging down his spoon.

Don't say stinking, Waldo.
You don't hear your father and I
say stinking.

Well,
it's a cheat
anyway!

'Why not go round and complain?'
said Waldo's dad. 'Sugden's make
those Hunny Popper things. Their
factory is only on the other side
of town.'

'Don't encourage him, Frank,' said
Waldo's mum. But Waldo wasn't
listening anyway. He had noticed
something very strange . . .

Waldo didn't finish his Hunny
Poppers. He dashed upstairs to his
room to have a closer look at the
message . . .

Chapter Two

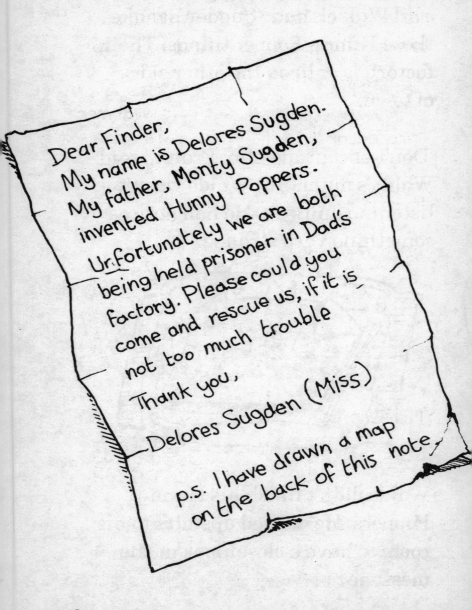

Dear Finder,
My name is Delores Sugden.
My father, Monty Sugden,
invented Hunny Poppers.
Unfortunately we are both
being held prisoner in Dad's
factory. Please could you
come and rescue us, if it is
not too much trouble

Thank you,

Delores Sugden (Miss)

p.s. I have drawn a map
on the back of this note

Waldo spent a long time in his room, carefully choosing the right clothes to wear for a daring rescue mission:

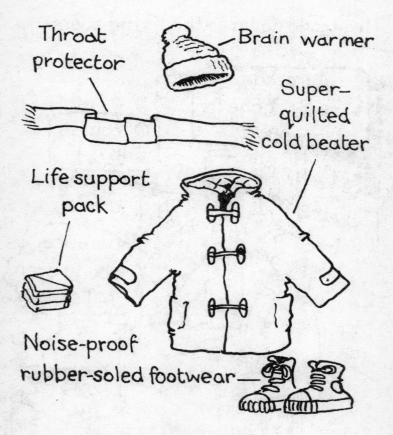

Throat protector

Brain warmer

Super-quilted cold beater

Life support pack

Noise-proof rubber-soled footwear

He tried to find his torch, but he couldn't, so the mission would have to be over before it was dark.

At last, Waldo was ready.

Ready for anything.

He strode down to the living-room.

Chapter Three

It took about an hour to get to the factory. It shouldn't have taken that long, but Baggage put up a struggle.

Finally, they arrived at Sugden's Cereals. The place seemed very quiet. Not a baddie in sight.

Except for one.

He looked ugly as mud, and mean,

and he was guarding the only way in.

Suddenly Waldo jumped up.

'Right,' said Waldo. 'After three.
One . . . two . . .

Chapter Four

. . . THREE!

Stopping only to check the traffic on
the main road,
Baggage

bolted

through

the

main

gate.

Baggage dived into the bushes, and
started to sneak towards the bins.

This was Waldo's big moment.
He walked up to the guard, with big
fake tears rolling down his cheeks.

Then Waldo used his Secret Weapon:

the
    sorriest,

      soppiest,

        saddest look

you've ever seen in your life.

Waldo had been practising it on his mum for years, and it had never been known to fail.

'Oh, go on then,' said the guard, 'but be quick, and mind you don't snoop about. This is private property.'

Waldo walked through the gate. He'd done it. He was in!

Now all he's got to do is find this girl and her dad rescue them, and get away without being caught.

Easy!

Chapter Five

You could say one thing for Delores
Sugden. She drew a good map.
Keeping out of sight, Waldo and
Baggage made their way around
the factory grounds.

They ran
across the
drive,

they tiptoed
over the lawn,

they edged along the wall,

until they reached the back of the
office block.

At last, Waldo was ready.

Ready for anything.

He strode down to the living-room.

"Mum, can I take Baggage for a walk?"

"Of course, dear."

"Notice, nobody ever asks me."

Waldo spent a long time in his room, carefully choosing the right clothes to wear for a daring rescue mission:

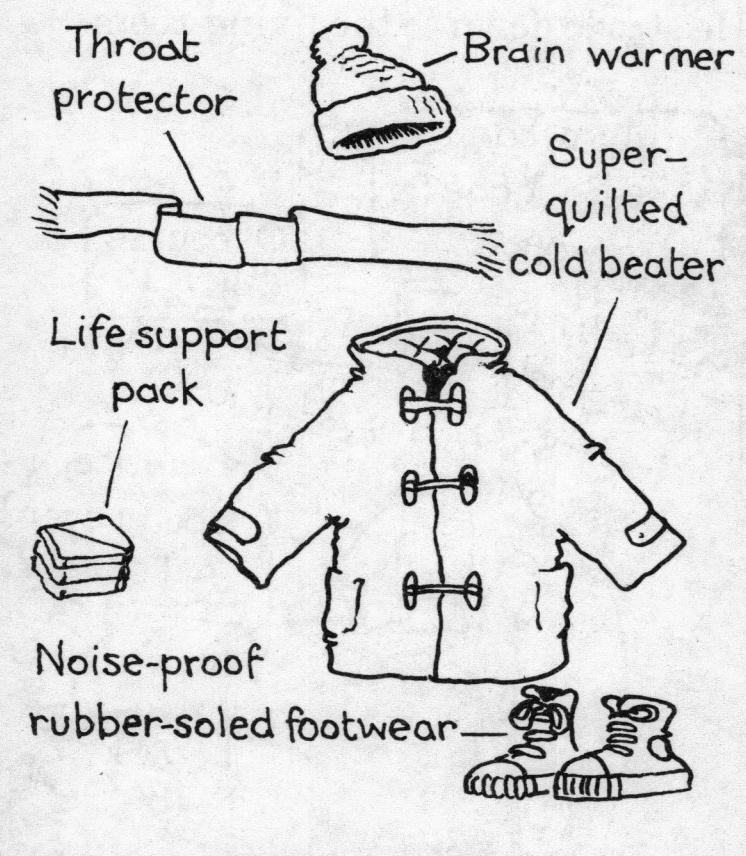

Throat protector

Brain warmer

Super-quilted cold beater

Life support pack

Noise-proof rubber-soled footwear

He tried to find his torch, but he couldn't, so the mission would have to be over before it was dark.

Chapter Six

How could Waldo know what sort
of nasty no-goods he was up against.

Stig Stubble had been a criminal for
as long as he could remember.
Which wasn't very long – he didn't
have a very good memory. In fact it
was his bad memory that
had turned him into a
criminal in the
first place.
He always forgot to
carry the keys to
his house, so he had
to keep breaking in. It didn't take
him long to start looking for other
people's houses to break into.

Stig wasn't all bad. But he was
nearly all bad.

Prisoner 2413819

Oswald Bingly was bad through and through.

He was only happy when he was doing something mean. And he did something mean about once every twelve seconds.

When he was five, Oswald had begged his parents for a pet. They said that they would get him something quiet, that was cheap to feed, and didn't need much exercise.

It took Oswald ten years to realise that he had been given a pet carpet.

It was on the day that Oswald's father had the carpet put down that Oswald started being *really* mean.

First of all he pulled his parents' house down, and built a supermarket.

Oswald's supermarket sold food for school dinners:

By the time he was thirty, Oswald was a school meal millionaire.

It was then that Oswald launched
his most ambitious product ever . . .

But on the very day that
Brekkysoggs went on sale, so did
Monty Sugden's delicious

crunchy

Hunny Poppers.

Brekkysoggs were a complete flop.

Oswald swore . . .

stamped . . .

and planned
his revenge on
the Sugdens.

Oswald put an advertisement in the
Criminal Chronicle:

**CRAFTY CROOKS WANTED
FOR MEAN MEGA-CRIME**
(Must be able to work weekends)
Apply to: OSWALD BINGLY,
SOGGYSTUF FOODS.

hard! used, 195

Oswald chose the meanest gang he
could manage.

Then he explained his plan.

Chapter Seven

Gentlemen, every Saturday Monty Sugden visits his factory.
But this weekend we will get there first. I will pretend to be a health Inspector, and tell the workers at Sugden's factory that there is a horrible, squidgy germ growing in the Hunny Poppers machinery . . .

Is there, boss?
Eugh!

Chapter Eight

Monty Sugden was proud of his factory, and he had promised his daughter Delores a guided tour. So, on that fateful Saturday, he drove her to

The first thing he noticed was the new man on the gate. The second thing he noticed was how quiet the factory was . . . And the third thing he noticed was that he and

Delores were being tied up by a big smelly man . . . Stig Stubble.

And that was how Oswald Bingly got Sugden's Cereals just where he wanted them – on a plate.

Chapter Nine

I don't know when you were last
tied up, but you can't keep people
tied up all the time. There are things that
even a tied-up person has to do.

Like go to the toilet.

Chapter Ten

Whenever Delores had to go to the toilet, Stig Stubble would go with her and wait outside the door, in case she tried to make a run for it.

But Delores had noticed something. In the toilet there was a small window, and through this window, Delores had seen machines

picking up tiny toys,

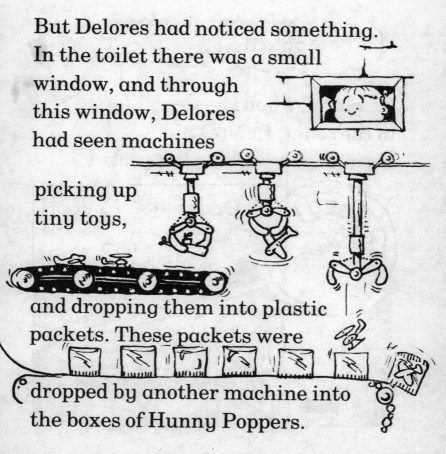

and dropping them into plastic packets. These packets were dropped by another machine into the boxes of Hunny Poppers.

Oswald's gang were still delivering Hunny Poppers to the shops, so that no one would suspect that the factory had been taken over by crooks.

So, if I can just get a note onto that belt —

Next day, when she went to the toilet, Delores hid a pencil and paper in her pocket . . .

Two days later the note landed in
Waldo's bowl, leading him to the
window of Mr Sugden's office,
where, at long last, he had come up
with a daring and brilliant plan.

Chapter Eleven

Waldo spotted an open window. He lifted Baggage through it, and then climbed in himself.

This is *so* undignified

They were in a storeroom, about six doors down from the crooks.

Waldo started to put his plan into action by frantically piling up boxes.

Stig Stubble lumbered into the hall.

Stig made a grab for Baggage. But the faithful hound shot back into the store room to see what Waldo would do next.

He didn't have long to wait.

As Stig came through the door, Waldo gave a mighty shove.

39

They crept along the hall until they reached Mr Sugden's office.

Waldo took out his sandwiches.

Waldo carefully placed all the bread butter-side-down on the polished floor.

THEN....

RAT-
TAT-
TA-
TAT!

M.SUGDEN

42

Waldo ran into the office and quickly untied the Sugdens.

Delores went straight to the telephone.

Could you get me the police please?

Bells rang,

CLANGALANG

bleepers bleeped,

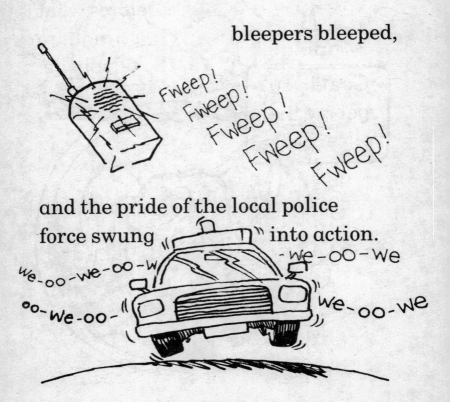

Fweep!
Fweep!
Fweep!
Fweep!
Fweep!

and the pride of the local police force swung into action.

we-oo-we-oo-w
-we-oo-we
oo-we-oo-
we-oo-we

BACK IN THE STOREROOM

Stig Stubble had come to his senses. At least, the few senses he had.

Stig ran down the hall.

Waldo, Delores and her dad burst out of the office just in time to see the crooks disappear round the corner.

Where's Baggage?

HOWWL!

Baggage, this is no time for games. We have to catch those two crooks.

Chapter Twelve

As Oswald's gang of breakfast bandits tried to save themselves,

Bingly and Stubble ran into the factory.

Baggage, you go with Mr Sugden. Delores and I will start searching at the far end and we'll meet in the middle.

Suddenly, there was a clatter
above them.

CHUGGA-CHUGGA-CHUGGA-

It
began
to rain
Hunny Poppers
They couldn't see.
They could hardly breathe.
They spluttered and thrashed about.

Then, as suddenly as it had started, the downpour stopped.

They looked up.

There, above them, was Oswald Bingly, smiling his horrible smile.

I think I have the upper hand, don't you?

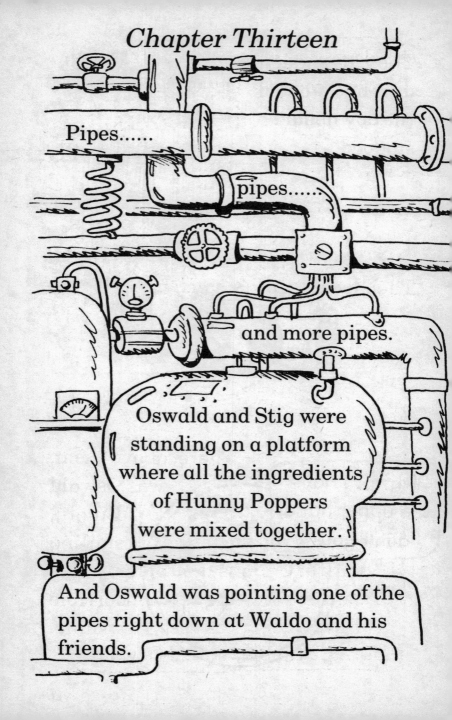

Chapter Thirteen

Pipes......

pipes......

and more pipes.

Oswald and Stig were standing on a platform where all the ingredients of Hunny Poppers were mixed together.

And Oswald was pointing one of the pipes right down at Waldo and his friends.

There was the gleaming
Soggystuf Cereals helicopter.
In the distance, sirens could
be heard.
'Hurry, Stubble,' called Oswald.

Down on the factory floor, Delores had noticed something.

On the dial behind Bingly's head, an indicator needle was showing danger. The honey-coating was under pressure.

The needle went higher . . .

and the police got nearer . . .

and higher . . .

and nearer.

STUBBLE!

At last, Stig Stubble remembered which button to press.

The helicopter spluttered into life.

And the police got nearer . . .

we-oo

and the needle went higher . . .

The factory door was still
open. As the helicopter
rotors turned faster,
drifts of Hunny Poppers
began to lift
and swirl in
the air. The rising
cloud swept up
towards Bingly
on the
platform.

Quick,
He can't see us
now – run!

They burst through the factory door
just as the police cars screeched
through the
EEEEECH! main gate.

Just as the pressure dial went:

Pioinng!

Bingly yelped
with surprise

as he became instantly honey-coated.

But it was too late. Flying Hunny Poppers were already beginning to cling to the sticky honey.

'It's not fair,' sobbed Oswald. 'It's not . . .'

Chapter Fourteen

Bingly, Stig Stubble, and the rest of the gang were driven away.

'You deserve a reward for all your hard work and bravery,' said Mr Sugden.

The Last Bit

Do you like Fridays? Waldo doesn't.
Every Friday, a van arrives at
Waldo's house,

and delivers a week's supply of
Hunny Poppers.

It's Mr Sugden's way of saying
thank you. The only trouble is that,
for some strange reason . . .

Just toast for me, please Mum.

Waldo doesn't want
to see another
Hunny Popper
as long as he lives!